When a whale falls
everything grows

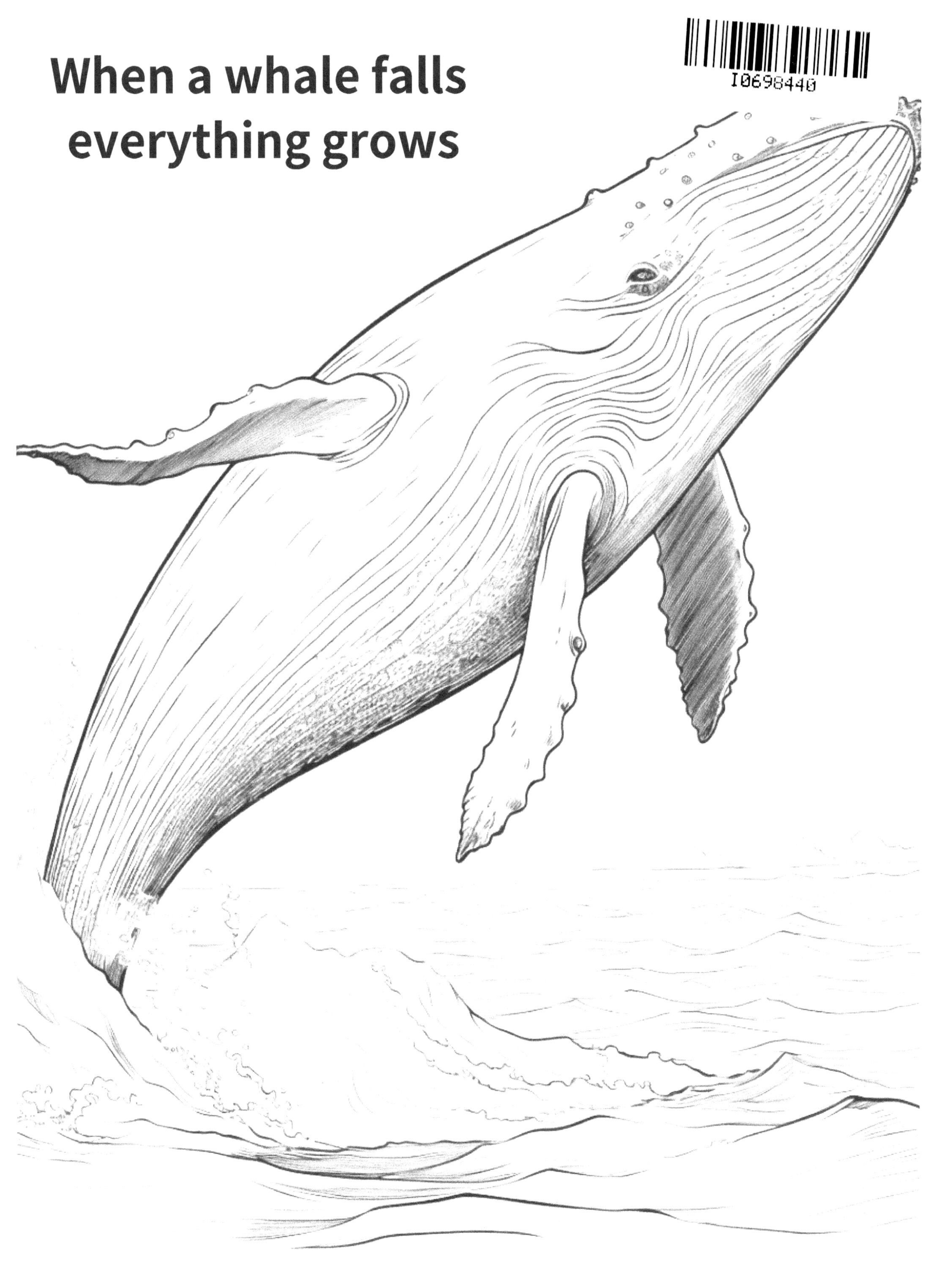

Common Dolphin (海豚) - Social Swimmers

Common Dolphins, recognized by their sleek bodies and curved dorsal fins, are social creatures found in oceans and seas worldwide. With a streamlined appearance, they are agile swimmers often seen in playful pods. Feeding on fish and squid, these dolphins bring energy and vitality to the waters. Their social nature and communication through clicks and whistles highlight the harmonious marine life they embody. A reminder of the beauty and interconnectedness of our oceans.

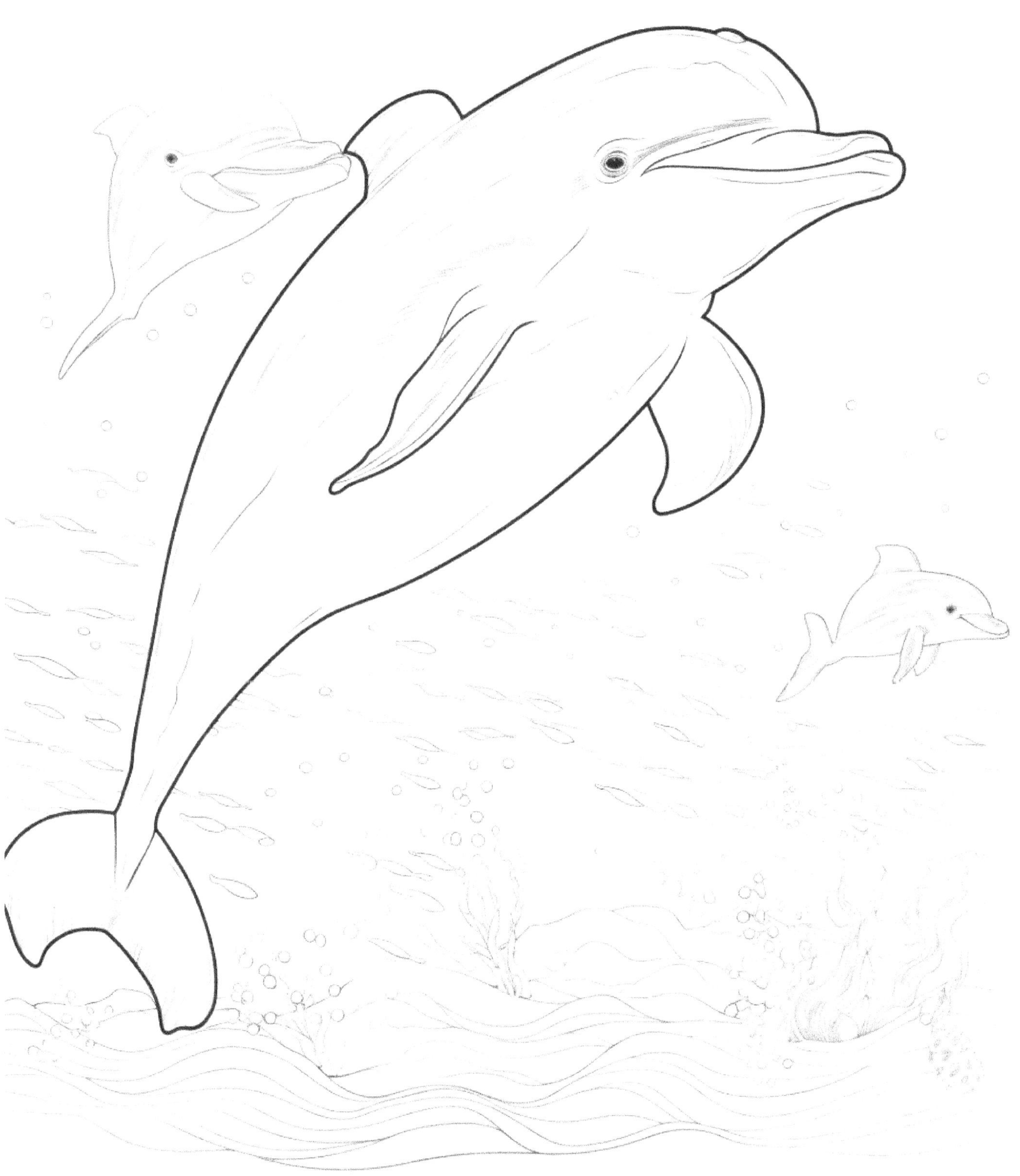

Sea Turtle (海龟) - Ocean Guardian

Sea Turtles, with their distinctive shells and flippers, are guardians of coastal waters. Found in tropical seas, they play a crucial role in marine ecosystems. Their unique appearance and diet, including jellyfish and seaweed, showcase their adaptability. Sea Turtles, known for nesting on beaches, symbolize endurance and resilience. Protecting these ancient mariners is essential for maintaining the balance of our oceans.

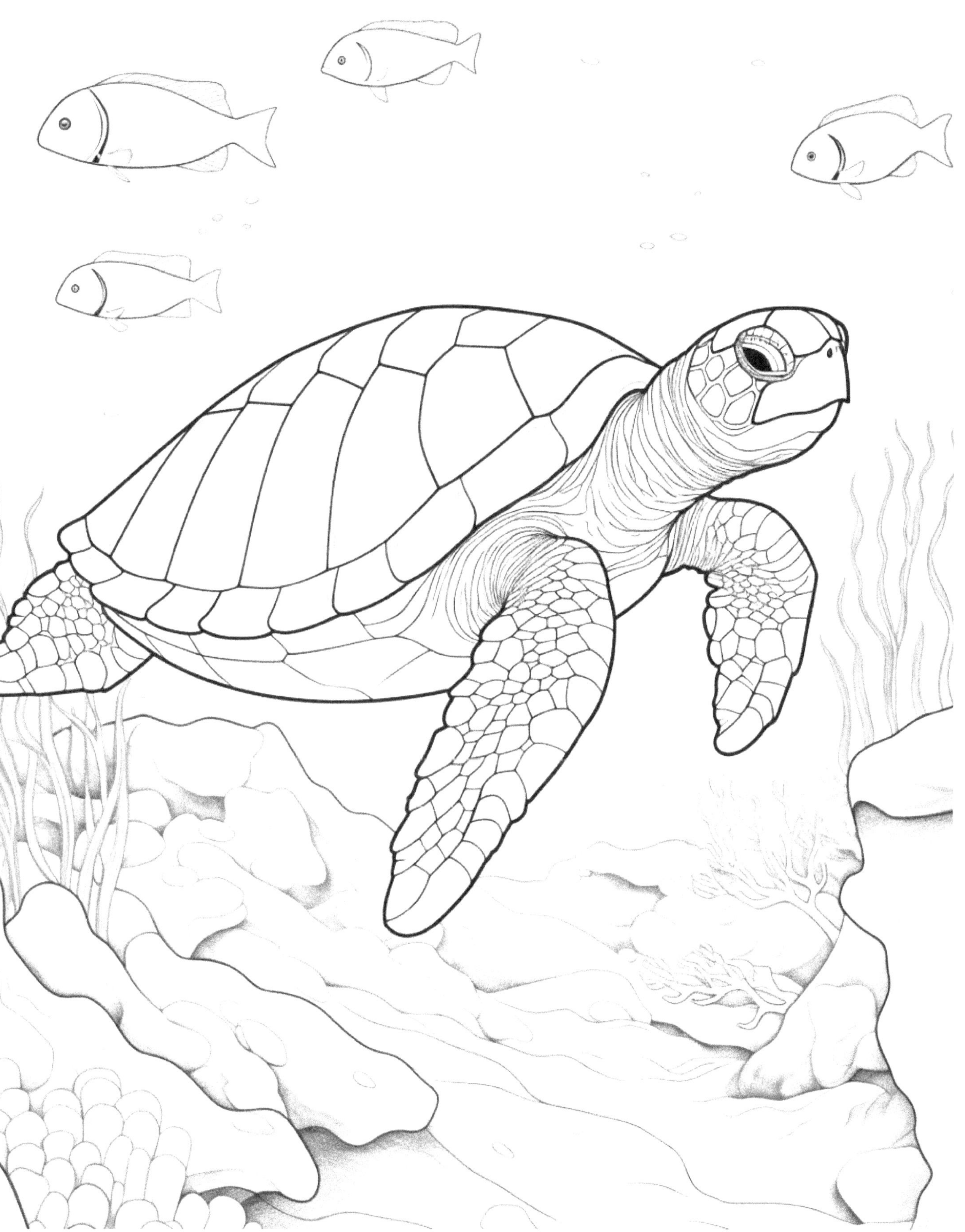

Clownfish（小丑鱼） - Vibrant Ocean Dwellers

The Clownfish, recognized for its small size and vibrant colors, is a fascinating inhabitant of the ocean. Found in the coral reefs of the Indo-Pacific, these lively fish are known for their distinctive markings and unique behaviors. Clownfish, with their bright hues and intricate patterns, create a mesmerizing sight in their coral homes. They form symbiotic relationships with sea anemones, finding shelter and protection among their tentacles. This partnership is not only a testament to nature's wonders but also a strategy for survival.

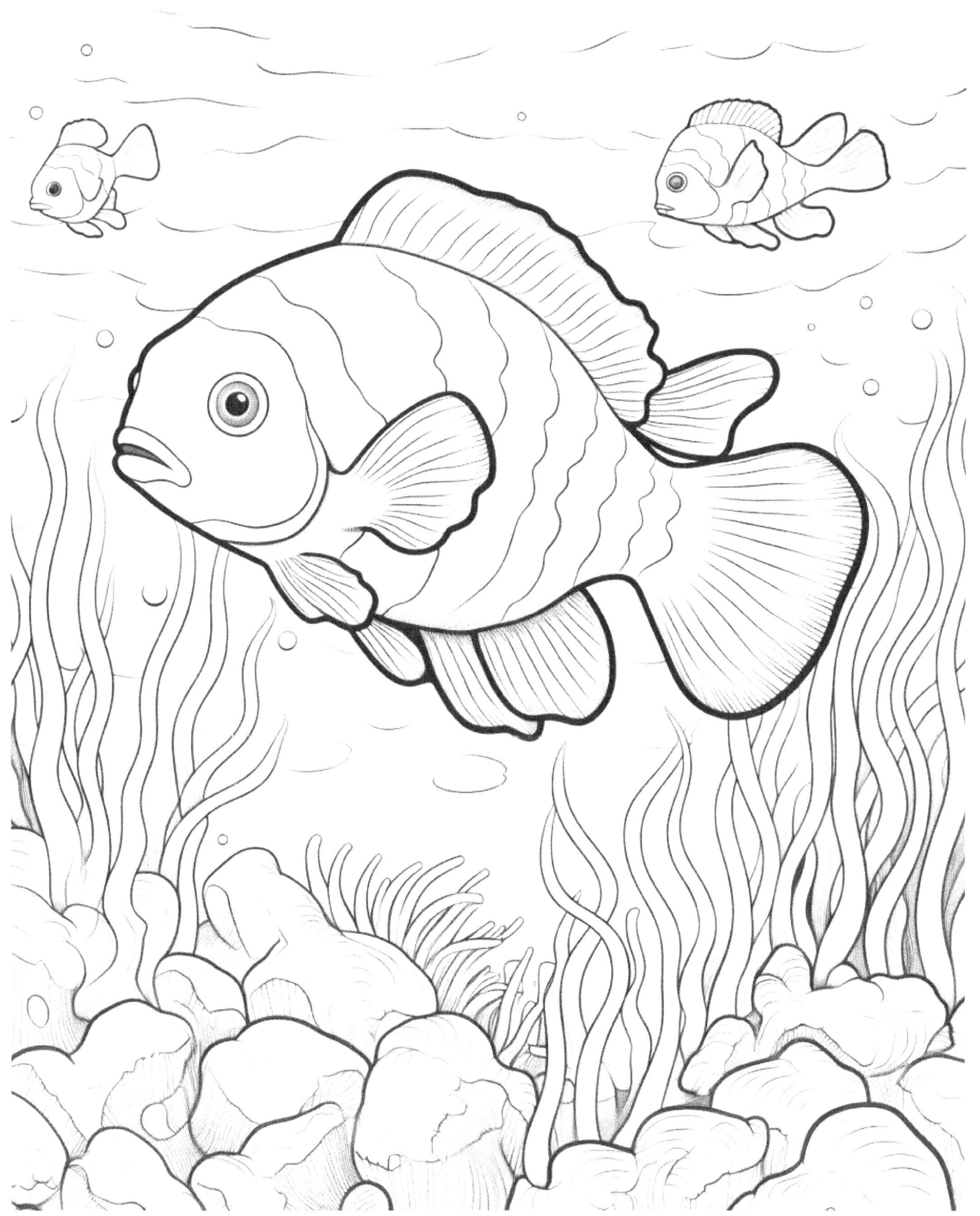

Coral （珊瑚） - Underwater Architects

Coral, with its colorful and branching or massive structures, serves as underwater architects in warm seas. These living organisms create vibrant reefs that house a diverse array of marine life.

Coral reefs are vital ecosystems, providing shelter and sustenance to countless species. Despite their apparent rock-like appearance, corals are living organisms that extract nutrients from algae. However, they are sensitive to environmental changes, making their preservation crucial for the well-being of marine ecosystems worldwide.

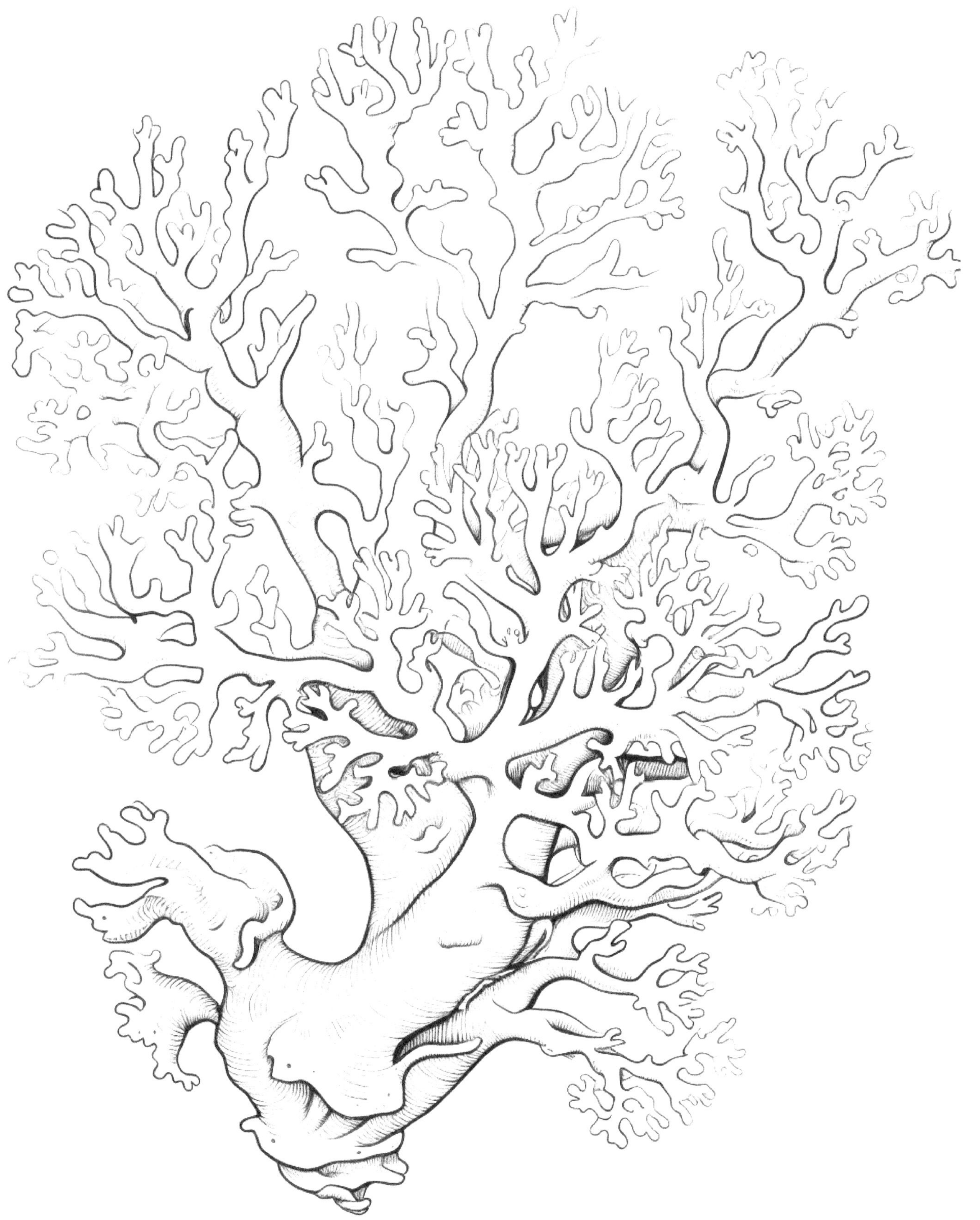

Hermit Crab （寄居蟹）- Mobile Shelter Seeker

The Hermit Crab, a fascinating crustacean, is a mobile shelter seeker found in coastal areas around the world. These small creatures have soft abdomens, forcing them to seek protection in discarded seashells.
As Hermit Crabs grow, they outgrow their current shells and must find new ones to accommodate their increasing size. This behavior gives them their name and makes them skilled scavengers along sandy shores. The variety of shells they inhabit adds a touch of uniqueness to these resourceful, adaptable marine dwellers.

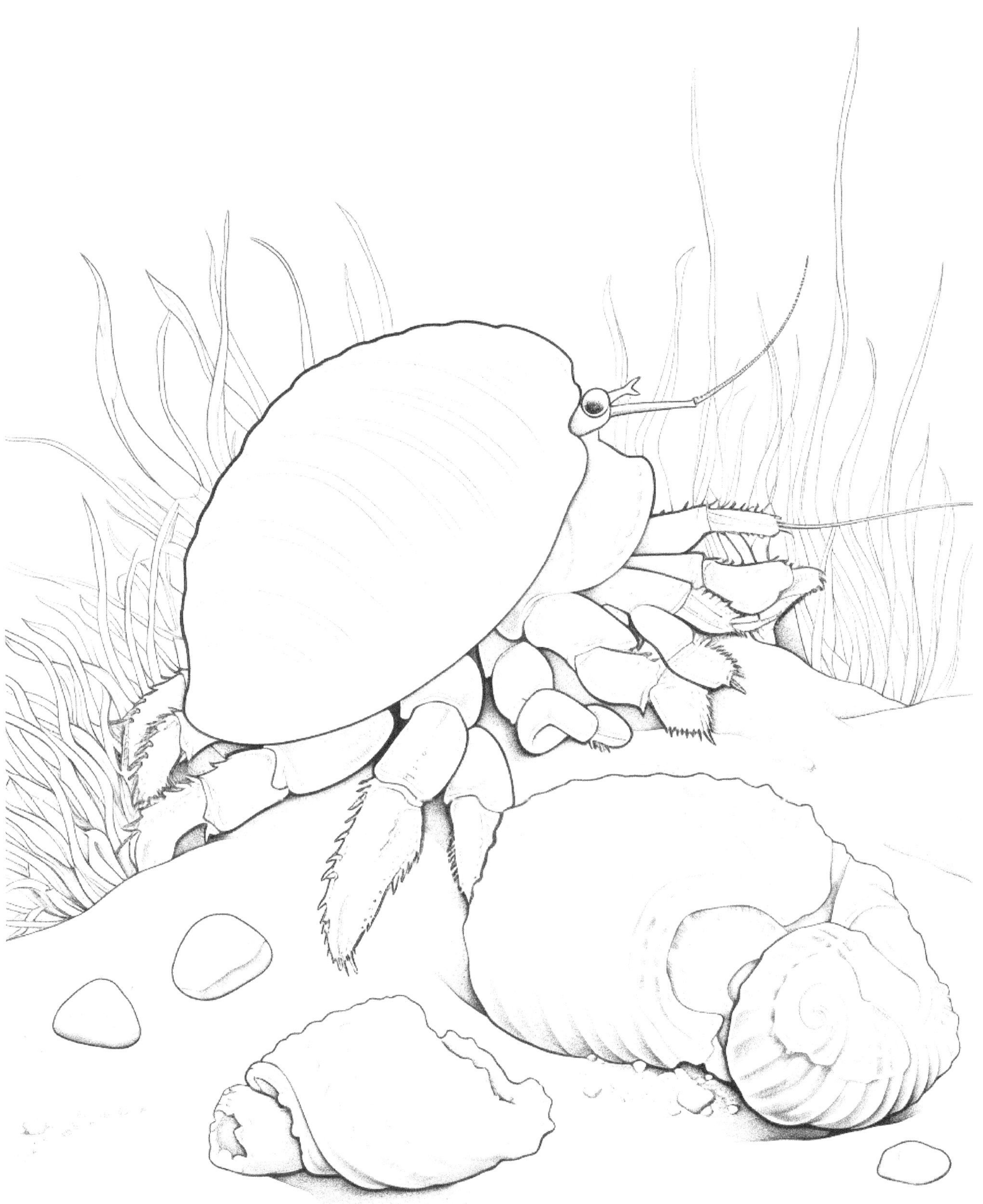

Seahorse （海马）- Graceful Ocean Dancer

The Seahorse, with its unique horse-like head and curled tail, is a graceful ocean dancer inhabiting shallow tropical and temperate seas. These enchanting creatures are known for their distinctive appearance and captivating movements.
Seahorses are true marvels of nature, as they swim upright and appear to dance with the currents. Their delicate fins and intricate patterns make them stand out in the underwater world. Despite their size, seahorses are powerful predators, using their elongated snouts to suck up tiny crustaceans with precision. Witnessing a seahorse glide through the underwater realm is a testament to the beauty and charm found within the depths of our oceans.

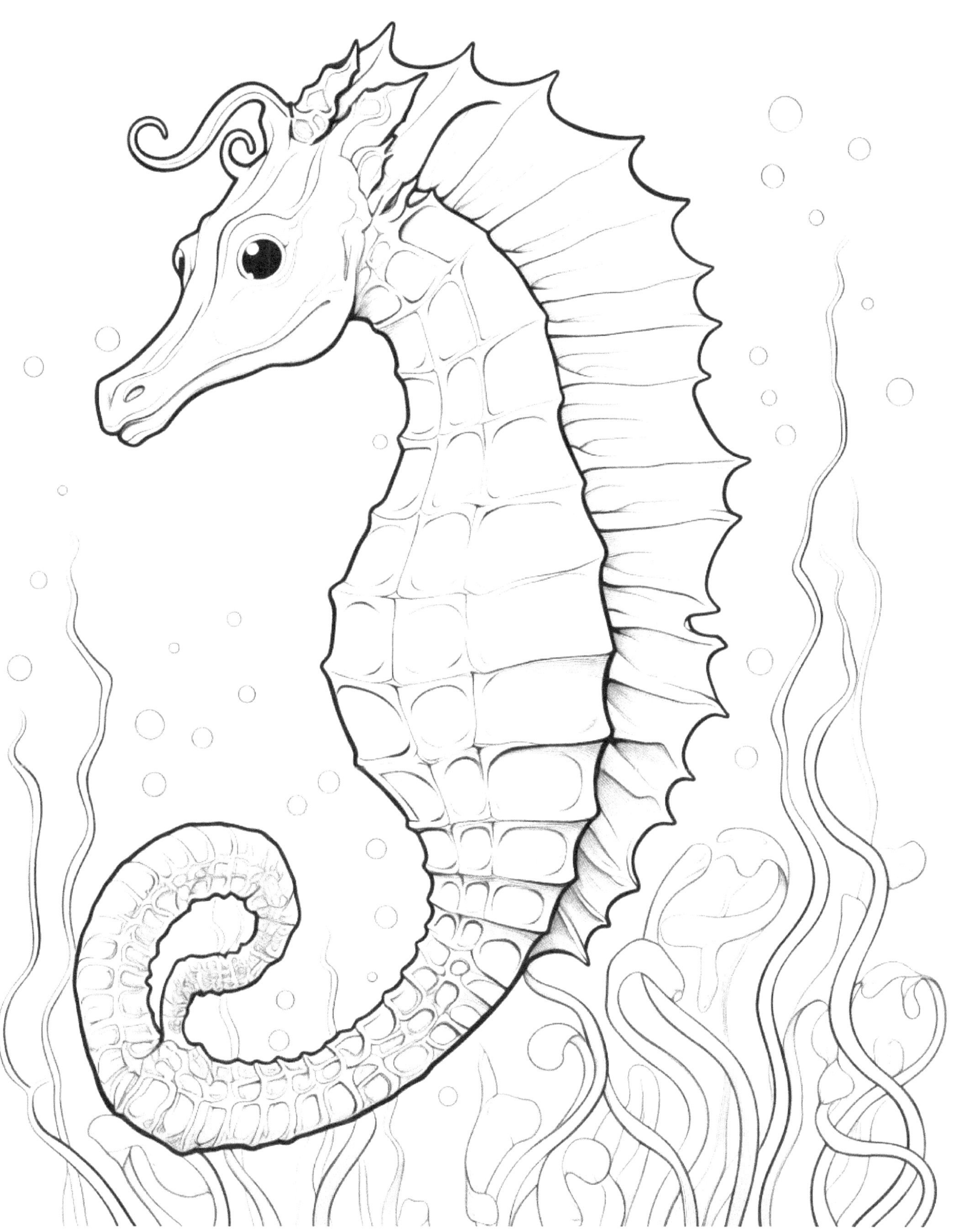

Jellyfish （水母） - Ocean Drifters

Jellyfish, with their gelatinous bodies, are graceful ocean drifters found worldwide. They move with the currents, capturing plankton and small fish with their stinging tentacles. Their translucent beauty adds a touch of mystery to the underwater realm. Appreciate these creatures from a safe distance in the vastness of the ocean.

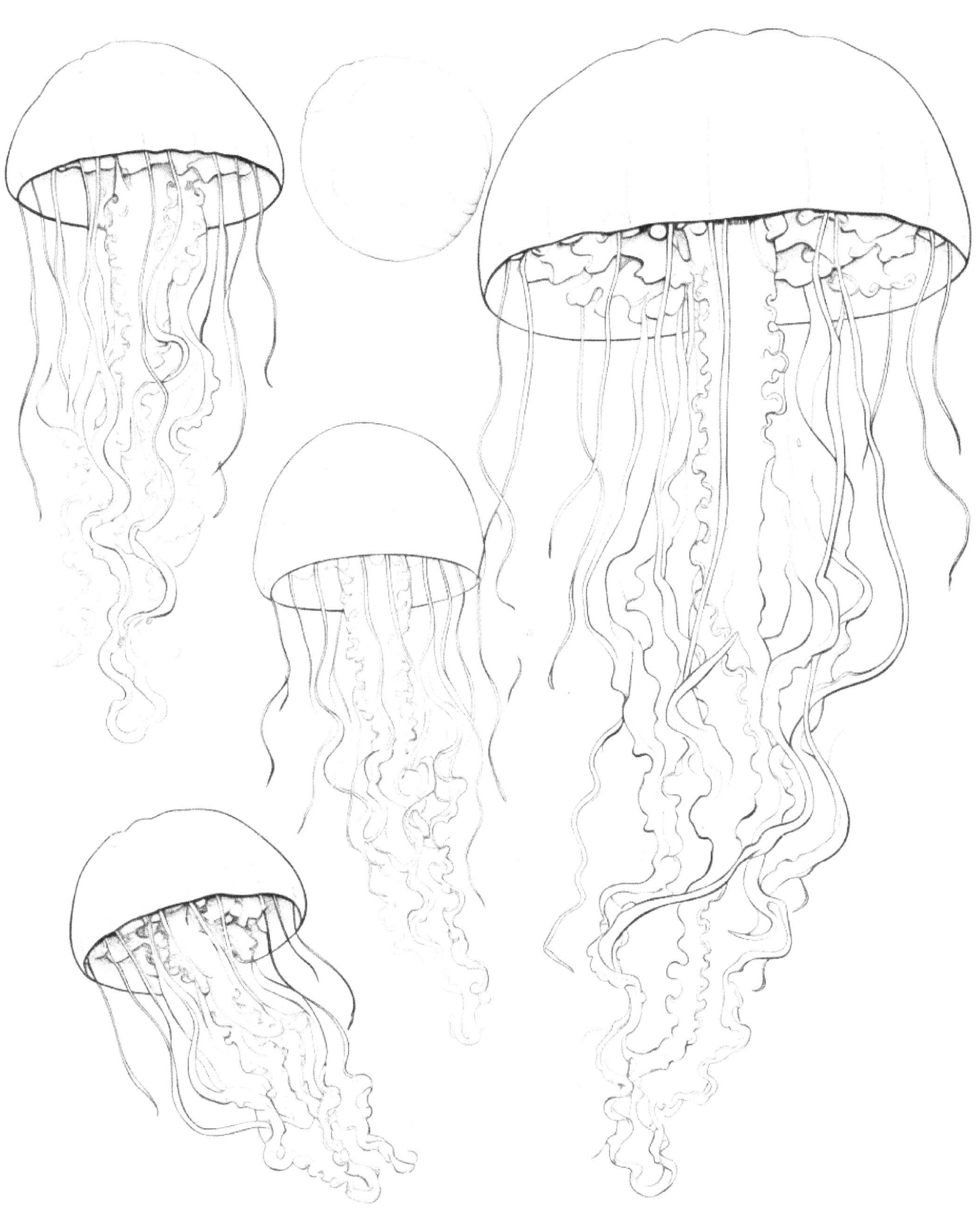

Octopus （章鱼）- Clever Ocean Dweller

The Octopus, with its soft body and eight arms, is a clever ocean dweller found worldwide. Known for intelligence and agility, it masters camouflage and problem-solving. A fascinating and adaptive inhabitant of the deep.

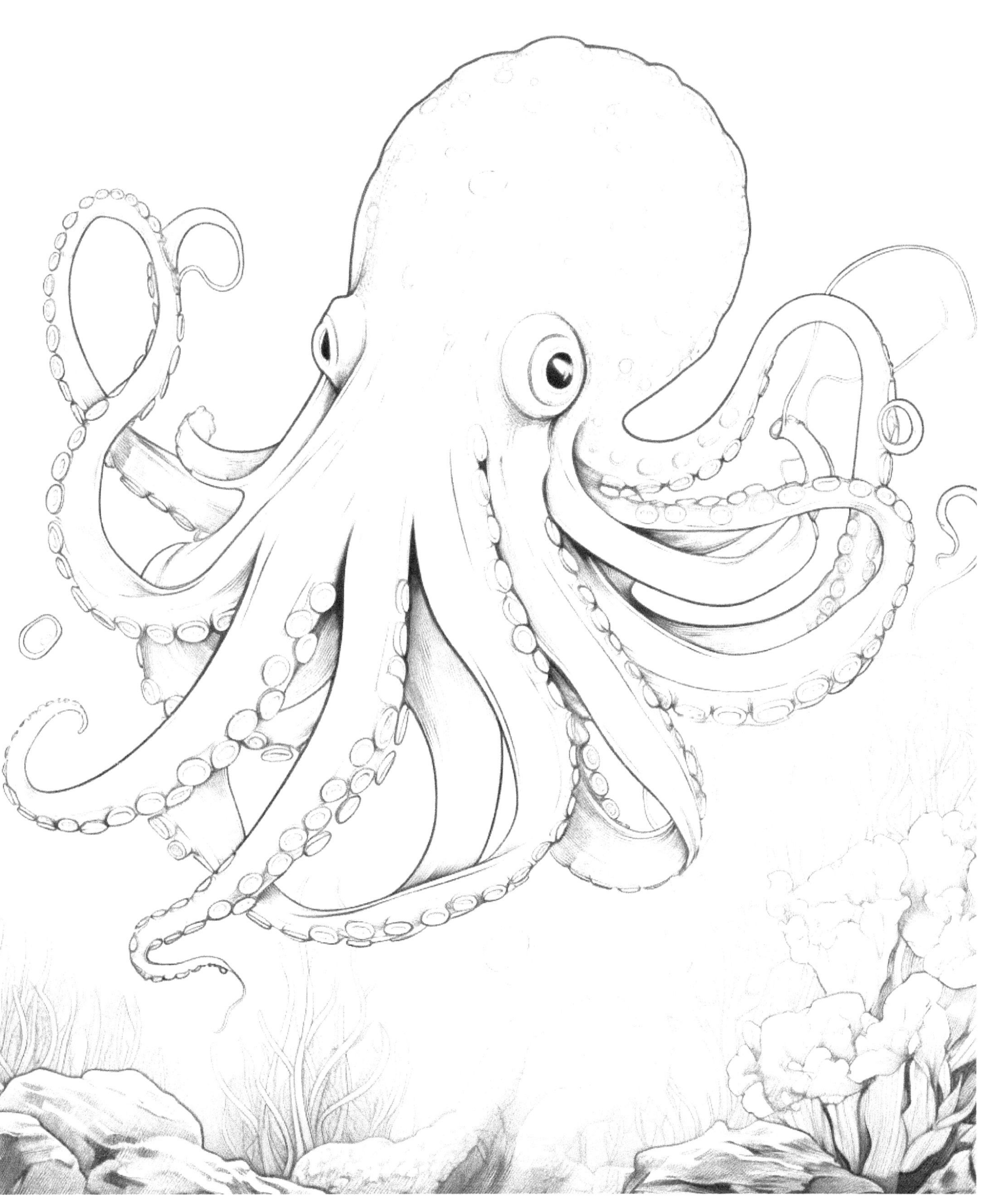

Squid （乌贼）- Swift Ocean Traveler

The Squid, with its elongated body and multiple arms, is a swift ocean traveler found in seas across the globe. These agile creatures are skilled hunters, feeding on fish, shrimp, and other squid, often evading larger predators with their quick movements. Squid are essential components of marine ecosystems, contributing to the intricate web of ocean life.

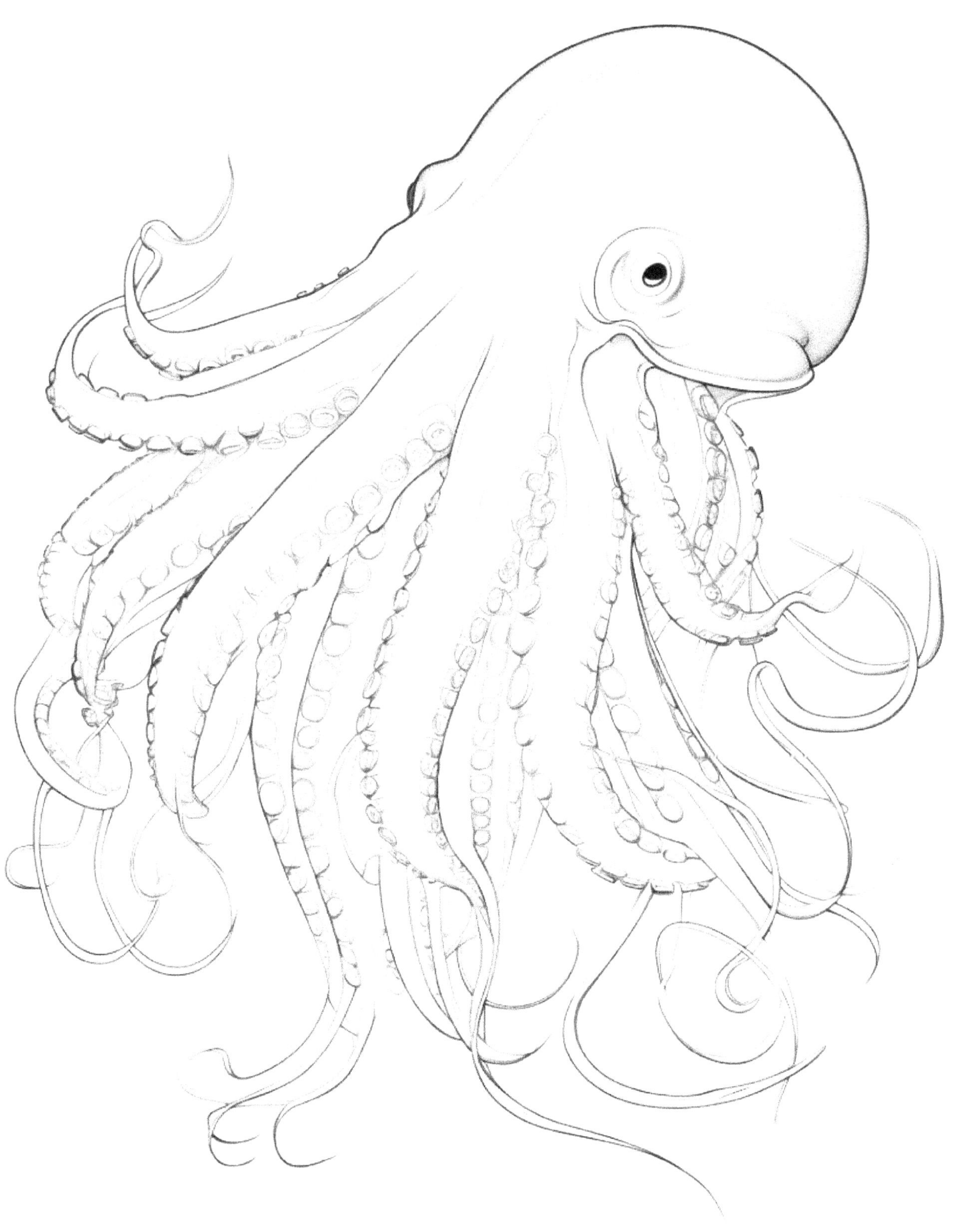

Lionfish（狮子鱼） - Exotic Ocean Royalty

The Lionfish, with its striking appearance and flowing fins, is an exotic member of the ocean's royalty. Found in tropical waters, these captivating fish showcase vibrant colors and elaborate fin displays.
Known for their venomous spines, Lionfish are skilled hunters, preying on small fish and crustaceans. Their presence adds a touch of elegance to coral reefs, making them both beautiful and formidable inhabitants of the underwater realm. Lionfish are a unique and captivating species, contributing to the biodiversity of marine ecosystems.

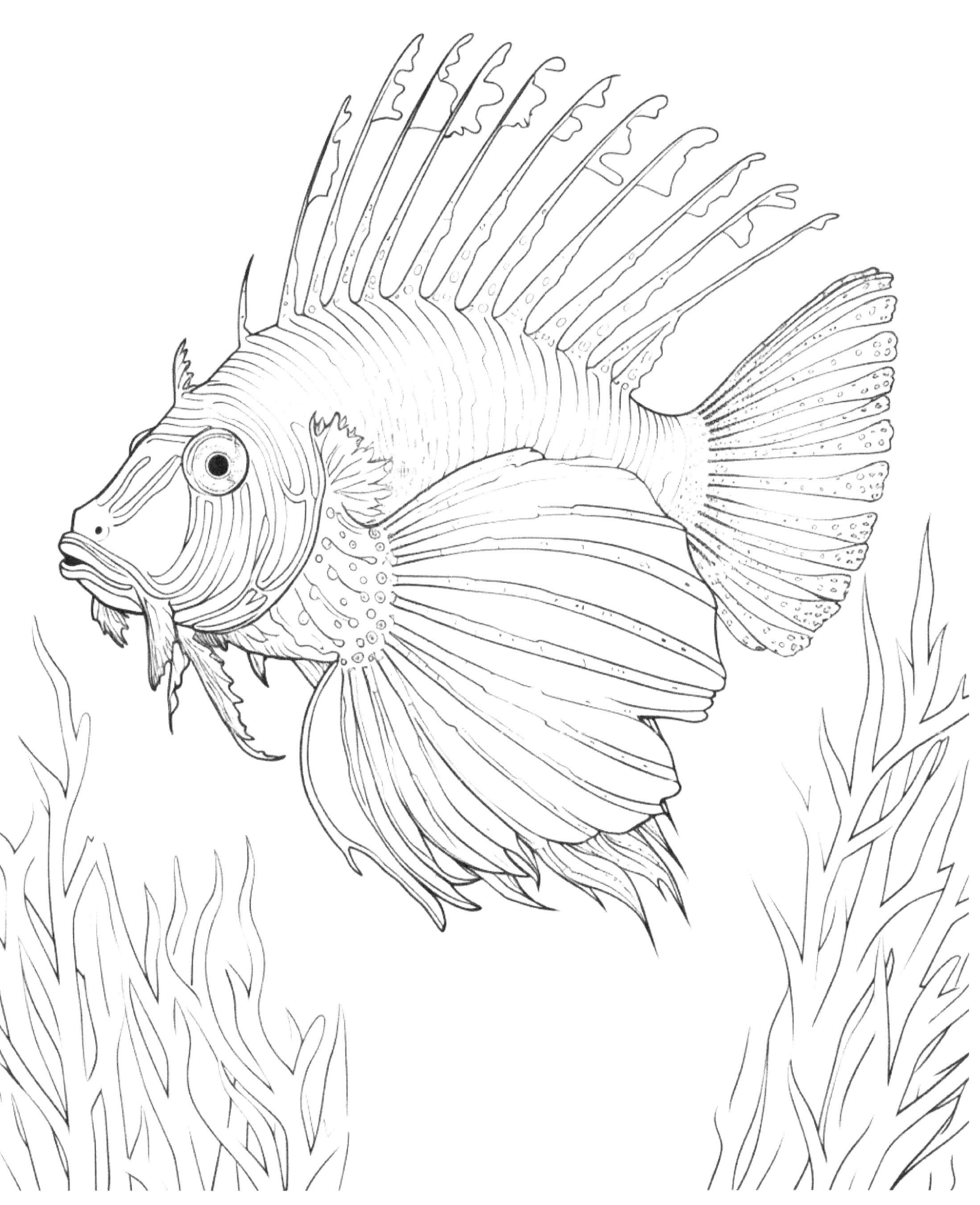

Tuna Fish （金枪鱼）- Swift Ocean Traveler

Tuna fish, with their streamlined bodies and swift movements, are prominent inhabitants of open oceans. Among them, the Yellowfin Tuna stands out with its distinctive yellow fins. Known for their agility, Yellowfin Tuna are skilled predators, preying on smaller fish and squid. Their migratory patterns and speed make them integral to the marine ecosystem, contributing to the delicate balance of ocean life. Whether appreciated for their role in fisheries or admired for their swift and powerful presence, tuna fish

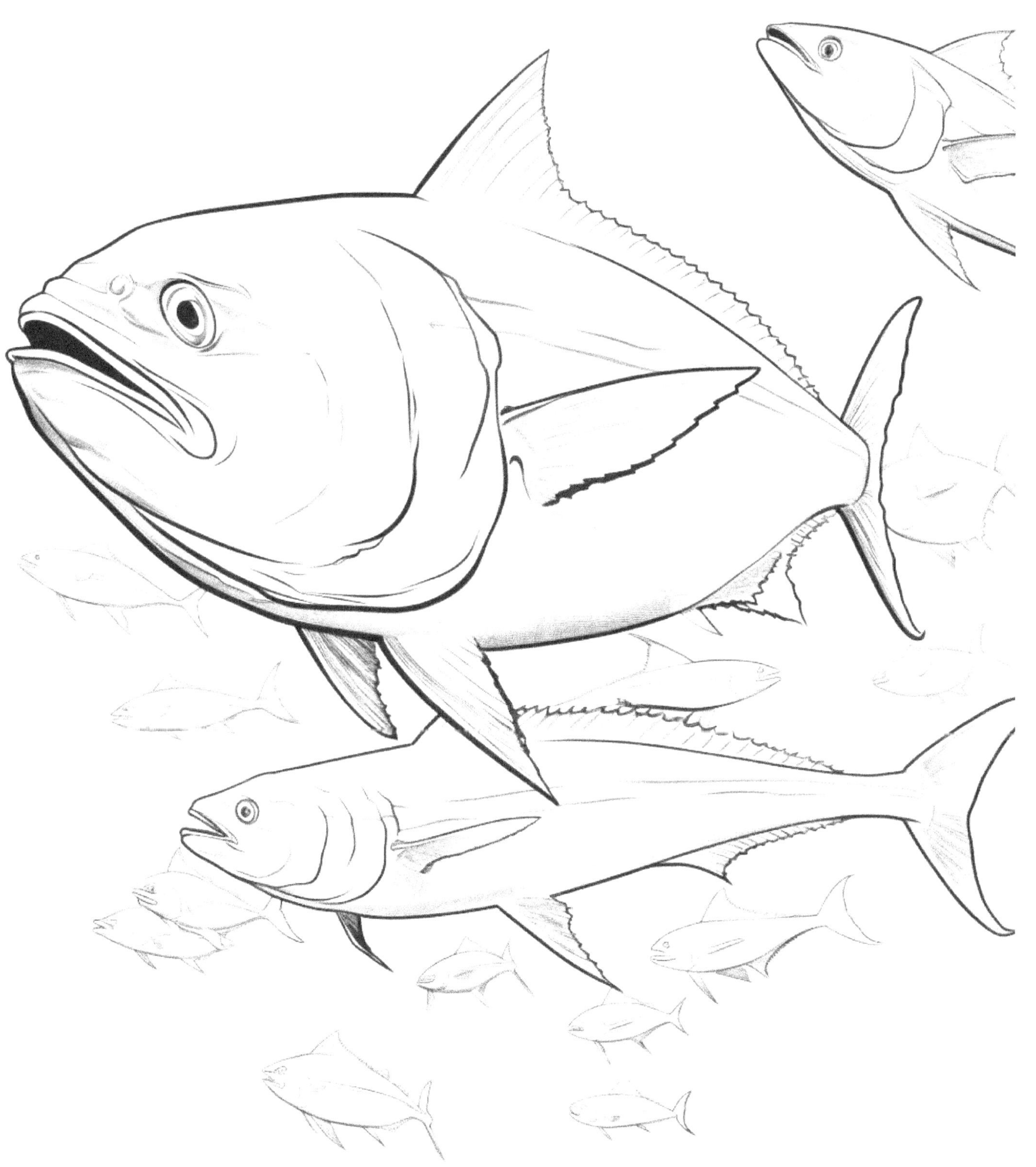

Grouper（石斑鱼） - Reef Guardian

The Grouper, with its robust build, is a guardian of coastal reefs. Found in tropical waters, it plays a vital role in maintaining marine ecosystems by controlling the population of smaller fish and crustaceans. A powerful and essential presence beneath the waves.

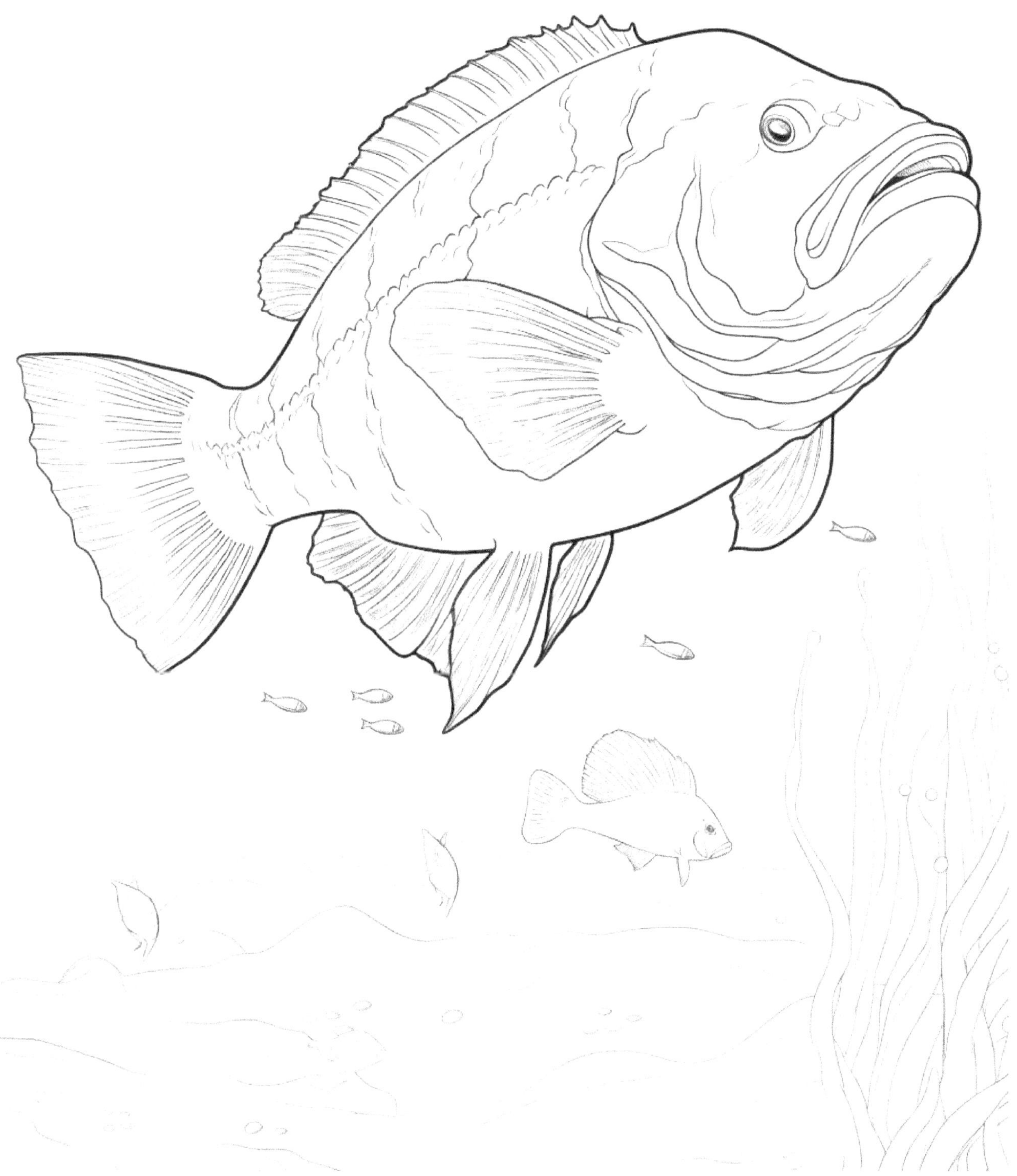

Angelfish （神仙鱼）- Graceful Reef Dwellers

Angelfish, known for their vibrant colors and graceful movements, are enchanting inhabitants of coral reefs. Their striking patterns and fin displays add a touch of elegance to the underwater world.
Found in tropical waters, Angelfish contribute to the biodiversity of marine ecosystems. They are omnivores, feeding on a variety of small marine organisms and algae. Their adaptability and beauty make them sought-after aquarium fish, bringing a piece of the vibrant coral reef into homes around the world.

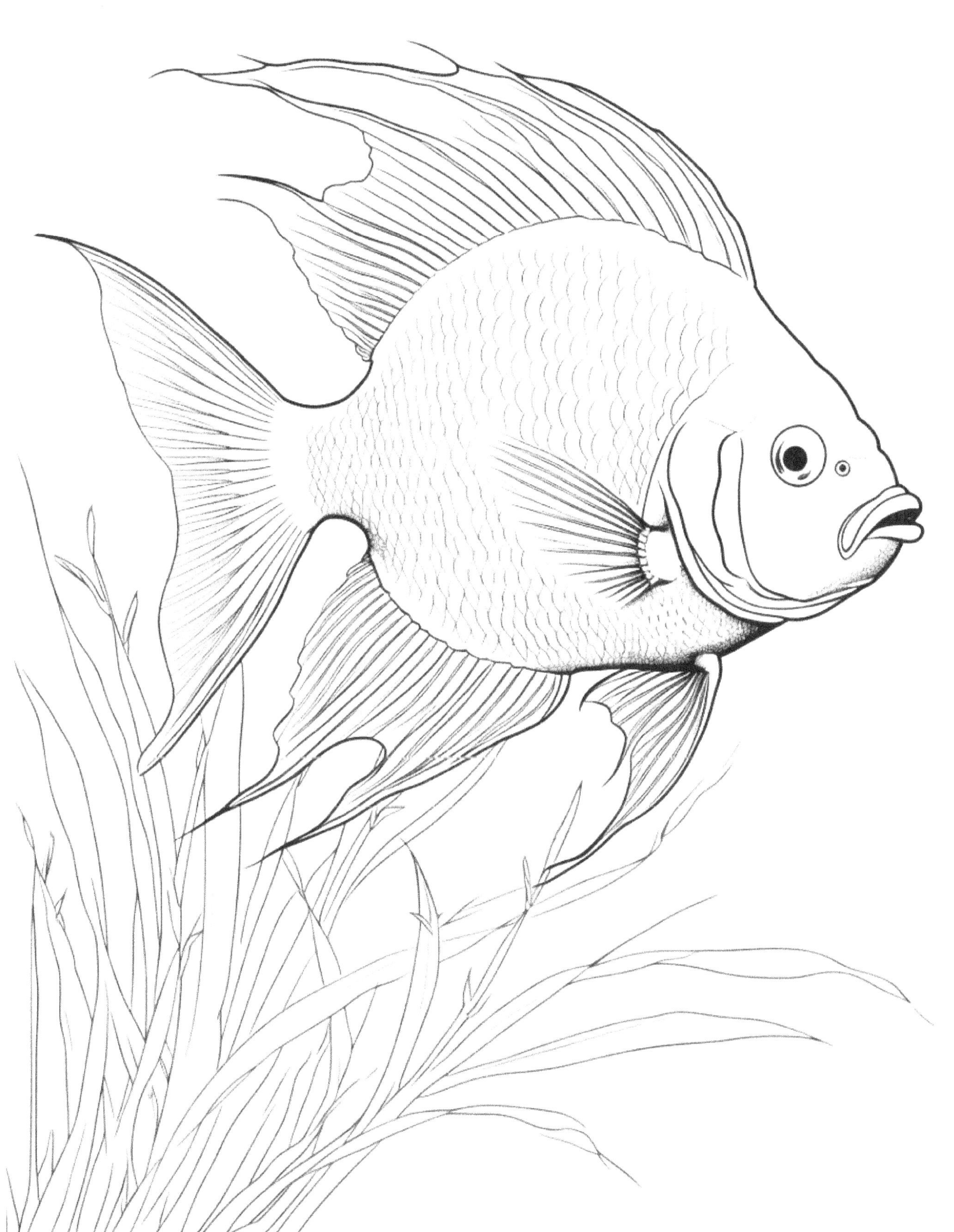

Great White Shark（大白鲨）
Apex Ocean Predator

The Great White Shark, with its formidable presence and sleek design, is the apex predator of the ocean. Found in various coastal waters, these powerful creatures command respect for their role at the top of the marine food chain. Characterized by their large size, distinctive dorsal fin, and rows of serrated teeth, Great White Sharks are skilled hunters, preying on seals, fish, and other marine species. Their streamlined bodies and incredible speed make them efficient and awe-inspiring predators.

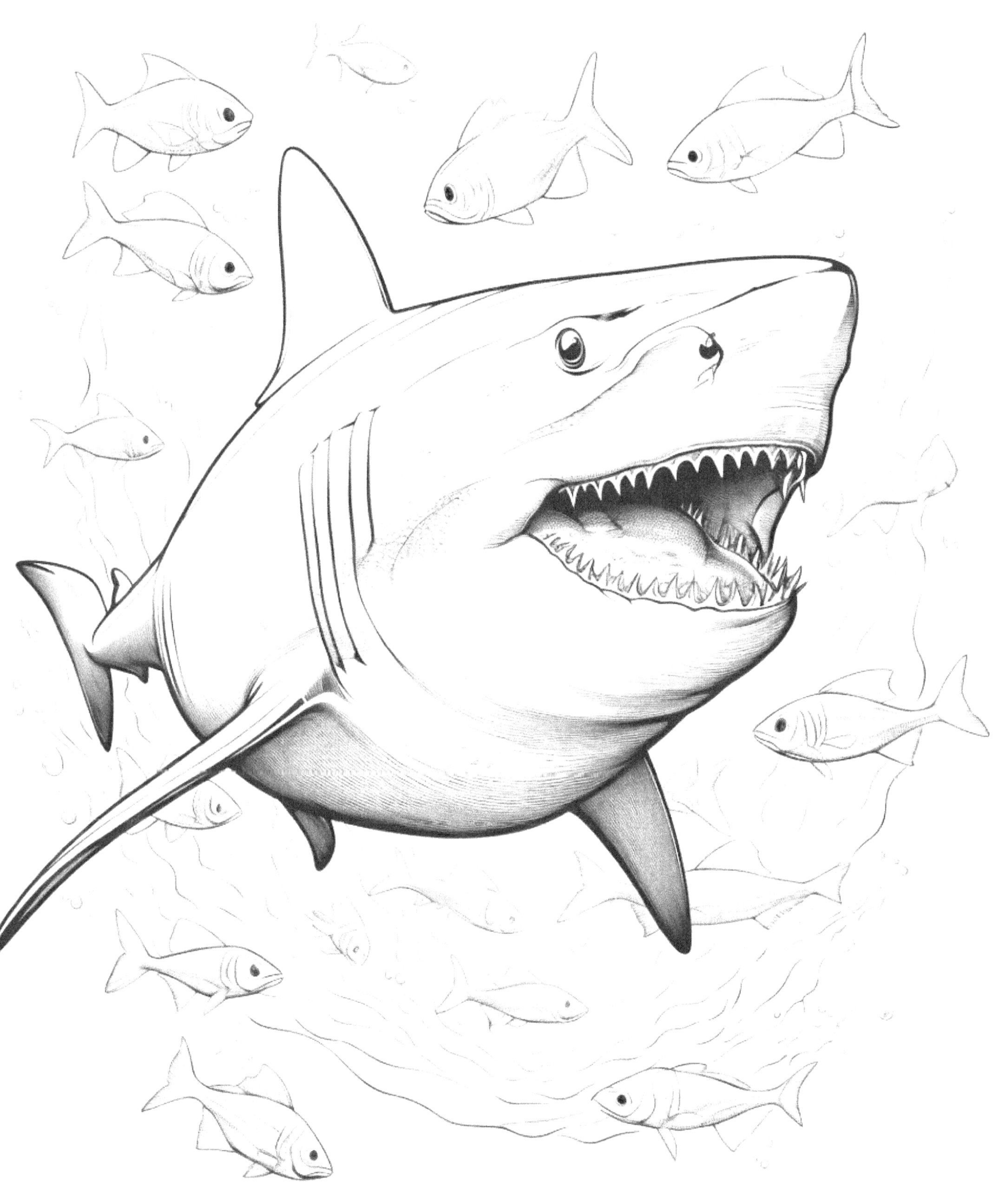

Starfish （海星）- Gentle Ocean Navigators

Starfish, with their distinctive star-shaped bodies, are gentle navigators of the ocean floor. Found in seas around the world, these intriguing creatures play a unique role in marine ecosystems.
Despite their name, starfish are not fish but echinoderms. They move using tube feet and are known for their regenerative abilities, capable of regrowing lost arms. Starfish feed on mollusks, small fish, and detritus, contributing to the balance of coastal environments.

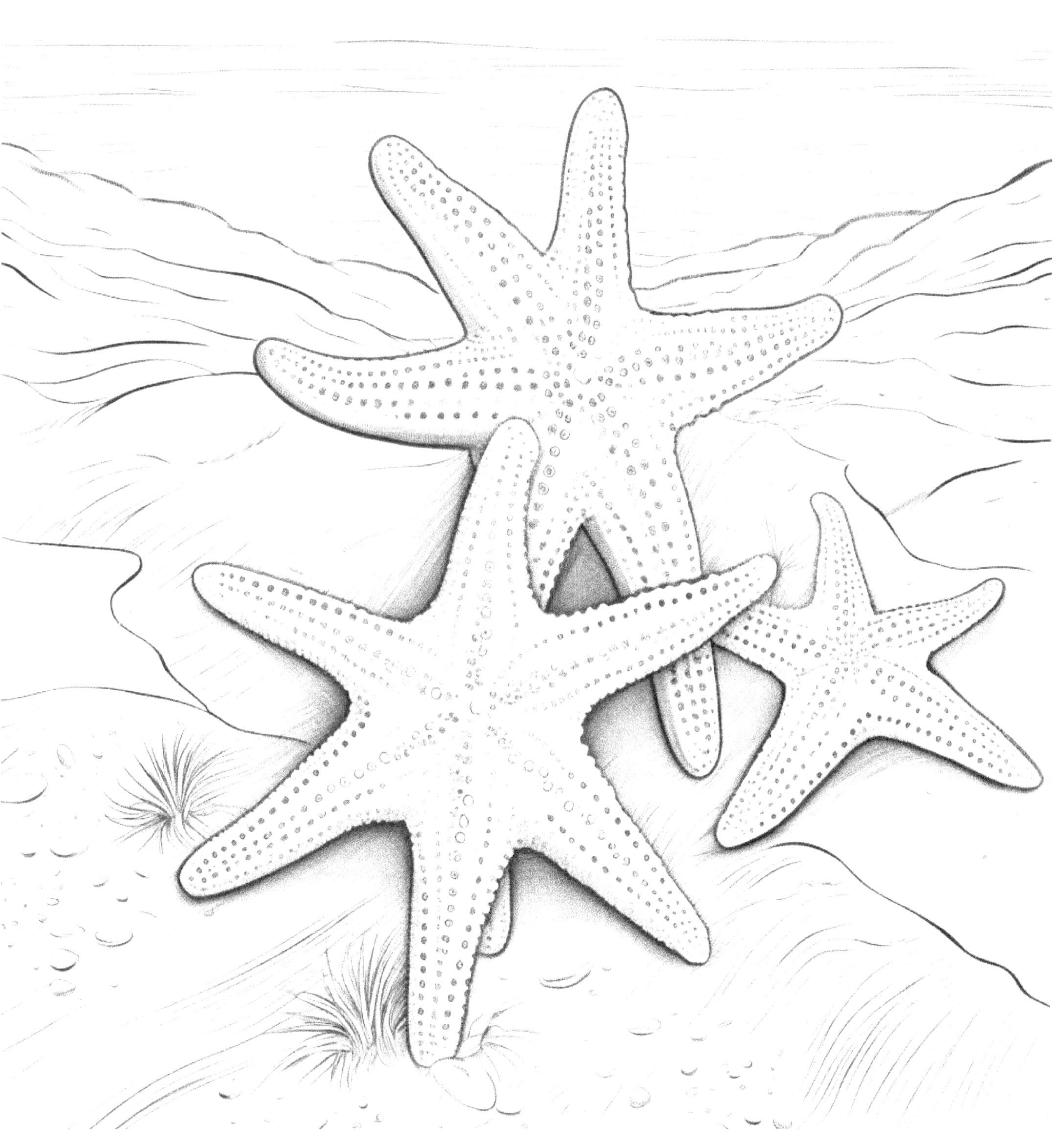

Pufferfish（河豚） - Charming Ocean Inflate

The Pufferfish, with its charming appearance and ability to inflate, is an intriguing ocean inhabitant. Found in tropical and subtropical waters, these fish are known for their distinctive ability to puff up when threatened. Characterized by their spiky appearance and unique swimming style, Pufferfish have a diet mainly consisting of crustaceans and small fish. Their ability to inflate is a defensive mechanism, deterring potential predators. While their charming looks make them appealing, it's important to note that some species of Pufferfish contain toxins, adding an element of caution to their allure. Pufferfish contribute to the rich tapestry of marine life, showcasing the diversity and adaptations found in the vast ocean.

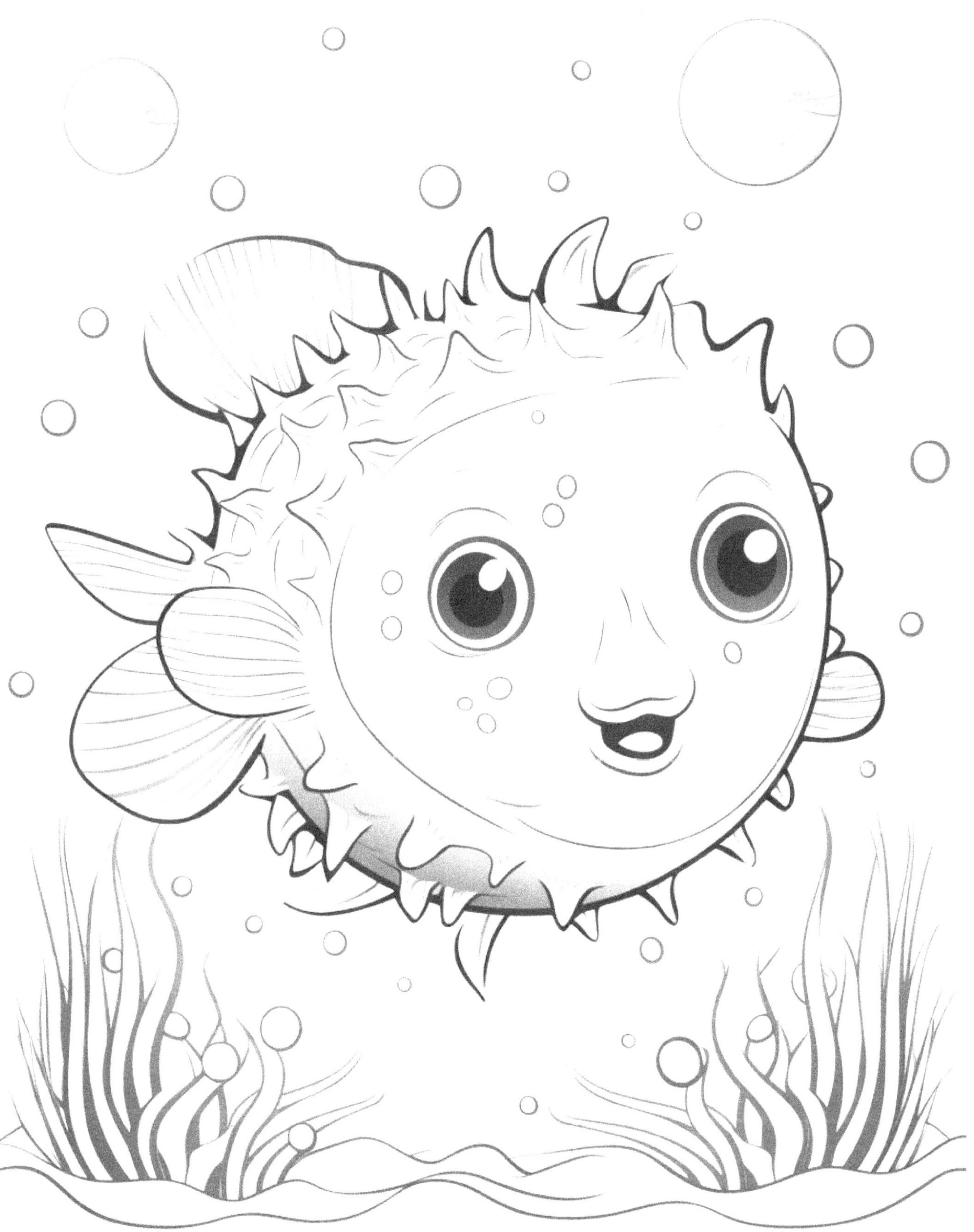

Barracuda(梭鱼）- Sleek Ocean Predator

The Barracuda, with its sleek and elongated body, is a formidable predator in the ocean. Found in tropical and subtropical waters, these fish are known for their speed and sharp-toothed appearance. Characterized by their streamlined shape and powerful jaws, Barracudas are swift hunters, preying on smaller fish and squid. Their ability to accelerate quickly and cover long distances makes them efficient predators in both coastal and open ocean environments.
While Barracudas are impressive in their predatory prowess, they also play a vital role in maintaining the balance of marine ecosystems. Their presence adds to the dynamic diversity of underwater life, showcasing the intricacies of the predator-prey relationships in the vast ocean.

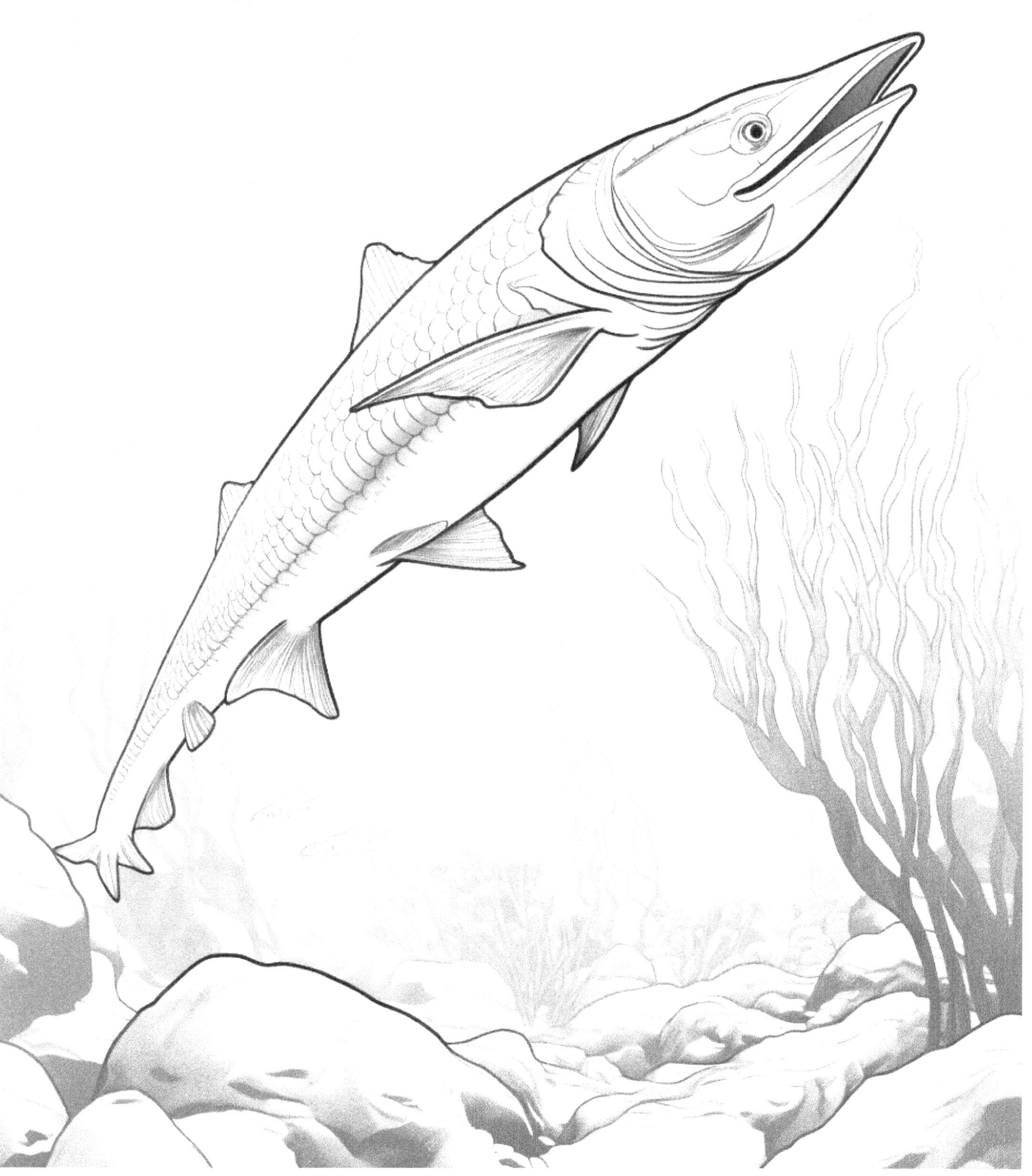

Sea Anemone （海葵）- Ocean Elegance

Sea Anemones, with their graceful tentacles and vibrant colors, are elegant inhabitants of the ocean floor. These marine animals, despite their appearance, are close relatives of jellyfish. Found in various marine environments, Sea Anemones use their stinging tentacles to capture prey and provide protection for certain fish species. Their symbiotic relationships, particularly with clownfish, create a stunning display of cooperation in the underwater world. Sea Anemones contribute to the biodiversity of coral reefs, offering both beauty and functionality. Their presence enriches the ocean's tapestry, showcasing the delicate balance and interconnectedness of marine life.

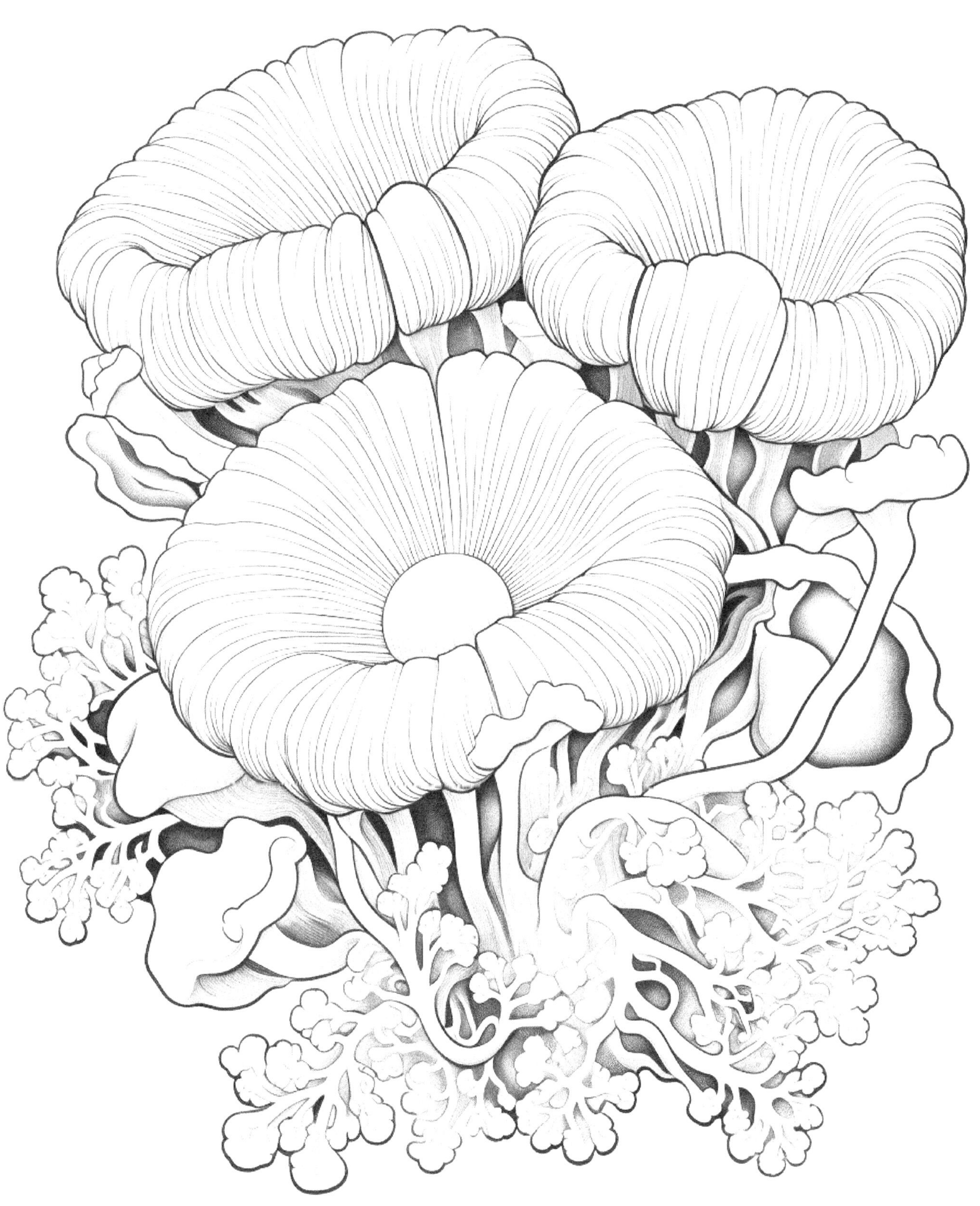

Protection of marine animals